# THE ETCETERA VARIATIONS
## POEMS FOR AND WITH MUSICIANS

DENVER BUTSON

THE BODILY PRESS
Amherst, MA

All poetry by Denver Butson
Copyright © 2024 Denver Butson

This book is set in Cochin and DIN 2014.
Book design and layout by Eliot Cardinaux.
eliotcardinaux.com

Cover art © Maria Saha.
Detail from *...the business of silence*
in *Dead Drop* Series
with Denver Butson, 2020-2021.
Assemblage of found objects and mixed media
on wood panel, 10" x 8" x 2"

Bodily Press logo designed by Katya Popova.
popova.space

# the etcetera variations

as always, for rhonda and maybelle

and for the musicians who help me
get this work off the page

# table of contents

| | |
|---|---|
| RETURN TO THE SILENCE (Lucian Ban) | ix |
| and WORDS THAT ARE ALREADY MUSIC (Mat Maneri) | xiii |
| REPEAT AFTER ME | 15 |
| from LET'S MOVE ALL THINGS (WHEN THE CROW IS REMOVED) | 27 |
| from THE SUM OF UNCOUNTABLE THINGS | 41 |
| IN WHICH WE ALL KISS SOMETHING SECRETLY | 59 |
| ENNIO MORRICONE IS DISSOLVING | 79 |
| LINER NOTES (*ASH* – MAT MANERI QUARTET) | 91 |
| IT'S NOT THE OLYMPICS | 103 |
| IF WE ARE NOT MIRAGES | 113 |
| Acknowledgments | 123 |
| Notes | 125 |
| About the Author | 127 |

# return to the silence
## Some musical thoughts on Denver Butson's poetry
## by Lucian Ban

*repeat after me now I remember blood birds the thin breath of a muted trumpet is what the sky above the bridge is the color of at this hour the first dead among us are blood birds agonies of red-throated blood birds repeat after me*

If someone were to ask me *what is improvisation?* I would send the above verse. It's hard to describe why, but for me, it has everything that makes improvisation work. There's the repeat, the fractal memories, the lines, the visceral quality, the looseness of real human language, the breaking of logic, the forward motion… As improvisers we're closest to poets in building worlds. And yet not all poetry is this close to improvised music. Denver's poems certainly inhabit a world where music and poetry breathe together. I know this because I felt it the first time we made music and poetry together. Playing music with Mat Maneri behind Denver reading his poems in a strange space on Atlantic Avenue in Brooklyn immediately felt free-flowing. I knew it right then: *this works*. I did not know why, but it did. And throughout the years every time we've gotten the chance to play through his poetry I've felt the same.

*was it meant just for you? because you will be dust. by the time this song. you haven't heard in ages. returns to the silence. from which it came. before you even have a chance to remember who sang it. once upon a time.*

Like all great poets, Denver draws you in. In his poetry, language is attacked from every angle and played with only to reveal itself renewed. It has been said that language is a barrier to the imagination – yet somehow Denver succeeds in breaking it down. We deal with the same in the practice of music – a complex language that is both the means for and the boundary of imagination. To bridge together poetry and music is rare. We're used to reading poems, or listening to someone read them, but the experience of improvised music with live poetry is a unique and daring proposal.

> *in which a man covered in ash leaves his briefcase also covered in ash on the sidewalk and walks away from it on the sidewalk and the briefcase remains on the sidewalk for days until it falls over ashes spilling out of it and birds descend upon it and rain descends upon it and ash runs like ink into the gutter and then the briefcase is gone and all that's left on the sidewalk are faint outlines of what was once something before it was ash*

The above excerpt is from Denver's liner notes in verse for Mat Maneri's *Ash* Quartet. He wrote them after we recorded the album. They work perfectly with Mat's unique and endlessly fascinating pieces. But I hear new music just by typing out the excerpt here. A measure of how profoundly Denver's poetry is connected to the possibility of music. Denver has read the poems that he wrote for the album several times live with the band, each new inception like a new album that could have been recorded live.

*in which the fifth player in this quartet is actually not a ghost but the act of listening to ghosts and to each other*

*in which nobody quite listens like this  listens not just with the ears but with everything that came before and everything that came after*

Great improvisations sound like composed music, and great musical pieces have the looseness of improvisation. There's no real difference between improvisation and composition. Words, as Denver implies, are like mirages. They mean something because we're conditioned to believe it is so. But we shouldn't forget they are closer to mirages than we think. There are no real bars in music. They only come into view as the music flows.

*if we are not mirages*
*what business do we have*
*disappearing*
*just as we seem to be*
*coming into view*

# words that are already music
## The poetry of Denver Butson
## by Mat Maneri

Denver Butson tells me the truth about myself. His words do not manipulate me, they do not force my hand, they do not trick my emotions. Clean and direct, I listen to his thoughts as if they were mine. I repeat after me. The music these words evoke is the truth about myself through his life experience. Denver has created form. I repeat after me. There is no room for mimicry. There is no room for gratuitous flourishes. There is no space confined. Openly, Denver tells the truth about myself. There is nothing to enhance, because in the quiet of his voice, there is me. Every vulnerability, strength, remorse, and joy slides through with the ease of Chet Baker. It is open, gives me the dimensions of the human experience, yet demands nothing. I whisper to myself, I repeat after me. How does this work. I repeat after me. Languages so genre-confined, yet Denver cannot be contained. It is the most free I can feel, when listening to the words that are already music. I feel free to confine myself to the truth of myself that is revealed so steadily, so beautifully, it provokes the silence in sound that is so precious to me. There are no twists of fates or surprise scares, just the inevitable magnifying glass to my own truth. I repeat after me, and before, and all that is in between. I listen. Listen. Listen.

Working with Denver Butson has been one of the most informative and fulfilling collaborations of my career. I can only thank him for his depth of understanding, and his friendship.

REPEAT AFTER ME

repeat after me this evening it rained I walked without a hat  the city like an arpeggio of loosened echoes  the sky like blood oranges  repeat after me  the sky like blood oranges  the sky like blood oranges  repeat after me  the bells are ringing   night is unraveling its dark threads  repeat after me   I am alone   a blush of blood birds  the piano music that drifts in from the backyards is as cold as a statue in the rain  repeat after me  when you kissed me long ago in the morning  was it this morning?  was it a thousand mornings ago?  I felt a flock of birds scatter into flight in my chest  I felt a café awning pulling up to expose a Matisse-blue sky   I felt a dancefloor exploding into dancers in a silent movie  dancers like unrumpled tissues their necks as white as ice

repeat after me   all my favorite shirts have fallen apart
I have a drawer full of shirts I can't throw away   each one
of them threaded with nights your fingers removed them
from my shoulder blades    a sleepwalking of insomnia
blood birds  repeat after me   there is a path that leads
through the garden to a secret place only I know about
and now you   we'll go there and build an evening of
Chinese lanterns   swaying in a cinematic breeze   you'll
kiss me with your country lips painted red for a city
night  the carousel will unwind into stampede   and when
the evening's over the café the carousel the lanterns will
disappear   and we too   repeat after me   in the ruins of
the railway station there's the shadow of someone still
waiting for a train   the scrawled initials of blood birds
in the taxi later you'll say *let's sing a song* and throw your
head back already singing   repeat after me   the night
kisses your shoulder blades and the moon staggers home
after the bars have closed   there's too much wine in the
sky above the city

repeat after me   the birds that fly out of the magician's palm are not the same birds you see later startled up by bus brakes but you can pretend they are   repeat after me once on Grand Street not far from the aviary called *Canal Street* we saw a mariachi band disappear after a truck went through the smoke from a hotdog vendor's cart I remember it was cold and we  blew into our mittened hands and you said *our very own mariachi mirage* and then years later we saw the same mariachi band again in a beer garden  in the Italian Alps and the trumpet player whistled and threw imaginary birds out of his fists and then they played *Orange Blossom Special* a Mexican Mariachi Mirage in Alto Adige playing bluegrass for Americans who saw them disappear once in  Manhattan  repeat after me   a childhood of flying blood birds  repeat after me  wind strips flowers of their petals  my fingers are wind  your clothes are petals  repeat after me  the clock is frozen at 3 o' clock *right twice a day*  you hear the counterman say  his words breaking like glass in sudden cold  repeat after me   a city's ledger of blood birds    an always of same blood birds a thirst of sudden blood birds repeat after me  *yesterday* is a word *today* is a word *tomorrow* is a word but *last week* is the beginning of a sentence  a sentence spoken behind a cupped palm into a leaning ear  *last week* the sentence begins and the ear leans in closer  already nostalgic for the words not yet spoken  repeat after me  the night is a book its pages are falling away like petals  like white birds like stars that glint  like windows of a distant city  repeat after me  there was a blurred conversation  a car alarm out there among the otherwise silence  there was sky above the canals the color of polished gunmetal  there were thousands of birds over the garbage heaps  a condemned sky of blood birds  and still we walked with braided fingers  and still we kissed until the sun threw itself finally into the sea

repeat after me  for a moment I knew everything or
thought I did  the sky was purple  and I said *plum*
mosquitoes exhaled like breath under streetlights
streetcars of grounded blood birds  repeat after me

repeat after me   I heard that the word *melancholy* escaped from her dictionary and smeared itself over her walls and mirrors   and I heard she switched on her television to drown out the sound of all the melancholy everywhere and never switched off the tv again   her ankles swollen from her finished heart   repeat after me   now I remember blood birds   the thin breath of a muted trumpet is what the sky above the bridge is the color of at this hour   the first dead among us are blood birds   agonies of red-throated blood birds   repeat after me   I cannot tell you anything else but that   not now   a suffocating of long ago blood birds   there was certainly a certainty of more   blood birds   repeat after me   pockets emptied of blood birds   among us once blood birds   supplications of blood birds   moon ascending over blood birds repeat after me  there was a barn and an old car in the barn  there were bottles someone brought in from outside  there were girls who were not yet used to their breasts pulling up their shirts  there were your lips on their breasts  there was a fire whistle breaking open the sky  there was a sadness you couldn't explain but could taste later  even years later on your tongue  that was decades ago and still you can feel its  hollow echo in your gut and still you can hear the barn swallows undressing silence in the rafters  repeat after me this is not my blood this is my blood on these walls on these walls not the blood the blood of my love of my love nor my mother's blood my mother's blood nor my father's my father's nor my brother's my brother's blood who splashed his blood who splashed his blood on other walls on these walls nor my living brothers' blood this is my blood this is not my blood on these walls on these walls  repeat after me   yearnings of ash-winged blood birds  yawnings of blood birds  a bouquet of broken-necked blood birds  the knifed guts of blood birds repeat after me  at night the river is the color of the inside of your mouth where your secrets sleep  repeat after me  a bell is ringing  the sky is kissed by neon  the sky is erased by neon  repeat after me  the statues have resigned  we need to find new heroes to put out in the rain  everything is an architecture of flown blood birds  repeat after me  why do I smell blood every time I read the newspaper  blood like ink on my hands  blood that won't wash away in bathwater? repeat after me there were wider skies  she remembered them  there were echoes that seemed to originate at the docks  or were they coming from the honeymoon suites? anyway she felt like she was falling  she felt like she was disappearing  she dreamed there were angels wings folded in her lungs  repeat after me  there's something about the color blue that undoes me  the way it holds out its hands and there is cold water there and then it's not  there's something about the words *her blue dress* that rattle the blackbirds in my dark trees  she felt like she was disappearing there's something about jagged rooflines and her dancing in her blue dress that finishes me off  renders me nostalgic in the middle of the night repeat after me  her blue dress train platform suitcase of broken birds  the whispered syllables of long-ago blood birds  repeat after me  me in my overcoat drowning  the inexact renderings of blood birds  repeat after me  that's not the river because it's not the  color of her eyes  that's not the sky because it's not the color of her eyes  those aren't birds flying up because they aren't the color of her eyes  repeat after me  those aren't birds flying up because they aren't unspelling promises she spelled out in night's secret classrooms  those aren't birds flying up  repeat after me repeat after me   already it's June what happened to May   blood birds  the carousel  the mariachi  the mirage sky  the color of airmail envelopes  repeat after me   this is not my blood  repeat after me those aren't birds flying up  repeat after me   the bell is ringing   night is unraveling its dark threads  repeat after me   I am alone   the sky like blood oranges   the sky kissed   the sky erased by neon   the sky like blood oranges erased by neon   repeat the sky after me   the sky after a stampede of carousel horses   a stampede of  swallows  repeat after me   was it this morning  was it yesterday   was it a thousand mornings ago?   repeat after me   repeat after me

from LET'S MOVE ALL THINGS
(WHEN THE CROW IS REMOVED)

let's move all things
(when the crow is removed, #20, for greg hershey)


let's move all things  invent hands to touch us
vagabond the language from ephemeral everything
while the drowsy flocks of books fall tepid
everyday  sir  etcetera  dreams like risen battleships
rise like risen battleships
like man electrifying liquor
like kings crucifying kings
everyday  sir  smiles like bled bells
like wheatfields set on fire
like a silk flag hoisted over the river's sighs

we all kiss something secretly

the sky pulls the bells   the sun dies
the moon pockets the night's agonies
the thief-possessors of dream
let's move all things  invent another language
vagabond the hands that touch us
the horses will gallop tomorrow
the countryside will suck the countryside
dry of sun  the world will dream of dreams

and memorize the invented names
of rivers and mountains
all bullets will burst into chains
all chains will break mouthing
the eternal language of broken chains
only we and the wind will recollect but only for a time
everyday  sir  etcetera  dreams
without so-called passion  a more violent passion
a word *violence* an infinite ritual of words
and precious  the language disdains language
madness of fireflies  explode like diamonds
like motorcycle drunkenness  a vertigo
of the drunk mouth  like walking numb
brushfires on the shivering tongue
these gymnastics of talking grammar
we all kiss something secretly
the sky pulls the bells  the sun dies
everyday  sir  only we and the wind

all bullets burst into chains
and chains break  while the veins loop
and loop into unbroken song

let's move all things, #10

vagabond the hands that touch us
vagabond the beauty of our catastrophes
our trains dancing
across the great floors of America
vagabond the accordion's last swallow
vagabond the final dreams of all those
who died in their sleep
the air between their lips
the gathered wind in their chests

*o she was lovely* I admit
mouth scrawled on her face
like a last thought
eyes like a brushfire
glimpsed from a car on the highway

vagabond those eyes
all it takes for day to break
vagabond those whispers
stuck in the throat
the pain we endure to laugh

vagabond the applause
that follows
our tepid performances

the neckties knotted for suicide corpses
the fingers that have picked chastity belt locks

o she had tremendous undergarments

vagabond the death sucked from her earlobes
the life huddled in her armpits

## Let's Move All Things (September)

everyday sir etcetera the wind whispers that it recognizes us
the trees hold out their handshakes the stars twirl around the sky
like bubbles in a windowsill glass everyday trains go through tunnels
like fingers through rings like scarves through a magician's fist
birds lift up like stricken punctuation marks

sir everyday I take my fistful of minutes and bet it on the wrong horse

if I weren't so scattered now sir I'd run around the block
in my new sneakers I'd show everybody how high I can jump
I'd learn to whistle all over again and I'd whistle
even though I can't really whistle

everyday sir the sun tells us what the moon did last night
how she sat in front of a mirror
lamenting the dissolution of herself

and we retrace our steps looking for something we've lost
even though we can't remember what it is we once had

we try to recall forgotten phone numbers
so we can dial them and hear voices
that belong to faces in photographs
we can no longer identify

I don't know about you sir
but I wouldn't mind a good fistfight about now
maybe a natural disaster to shake things up
I don't know about you
but sometimes it all seems like squealing car tires
with no crash at the end

we wait with faces squinched up
shoulders raised – for what?
I don't know sir.

## Let's Move All Things (September again)

sir. the sky bursts open. every night. like a pomegranate.
spilling. its dark seeds over the city. the moon laments.
the bowed heads. of sunflowers. and we struggle. sir.
under the infinite weight. of our eyelashes. and sir.
of course we remember. the day's sun. like the sun.
in a poem. by Octavio Paz. like the sun in a Miró painting.
it's September again. sir. time to begin. drying bones.
for winter's soups. time to start saying sir. what our tongues.
have been trying to convince us. all along. to say. what we
know. is unsayable.

## when the crow is removed (over twenty years since)

everyday sir every day madam everyday you etcetera
dreams like screaming children  dreams like fallen bombs
dreams like tents choked by smoke  dreams sir
dreams madam  dreams you   I spoke to Joe
yesterday it's been a month or two since his wife died
I asked him how he is doing
and he said *you know the emptiness  the emptiness*
I spoke to Bob the other day
his wife fell last week  gashed open her head
refused to go in the ambulance to the hospital
Bob said *I can't make her do anything   it would break her*
he stayed up all night to make sure she was still breathing
changed her head bandage in the morning
sir   madam   you
I saw a man hold up his headless baby  on my phone
I saw a mother digging with her fingernails
through stone to find any parts of her children
that might be left  on my phone
I saw a grandfather carrying a plastic bag
weighted by the ash and dust
he scooped up from the debris
because it might be what's left of his family
on my phone sir  on my phone madam  on my phone you

I saw a boy begging his dead father to wake up
everyday  on my phone
everyday  I walk along the water
I sit by the water  the same tern comes and sits in front of me
on an abutment  sometimes it has a fish it its mouth
and laughs around the fish through its beak
helicopters go over carrying bankers and arms dealers
bankers and advertisers  bankers and war peddlers
back from the Hamptons or back from meetings in
Washington  or Philadelphia  sometimes the President
with decoy helicopters and machine gun boats
in the water  and once long ago the Pope
I was on the phone with my father
when my father was still alive
I describe to him the fire boats  the Coast Guard boats
the police SUVs  the motorcade
across the water in Manhattan
all with the Pope in it
my father said *you'll never forget this*
and I might have already if he hadn't said that
all the guns  all the helicopters
a gunboat went by and I locked eyes
with a soldier pointing an M16 right at me
on the pier with my book of haikus
and my thermos of coffee

sir madam  you   one country is bombing civilians
in neighborhoods and we are calling it an *outrage*
and another country is bombing families in tents
families in their apartment buildings  hospitals
universities  grade schools and we are saying
that it is *self-defense*  I don't know about you sir
I don't know about you madam
I don't know about you  you
but I can't sleep with all the bombing
even though it is halfway across the world
and if I do sleep   I wake up and remember it
that this is what was going on while I was sleeping
and I ask for forgiveness
for the luxury of sleep  the luxury of dream
the luxury of waking up  and coffee
and sitting on the stoop
and listening to Lily next door
whose memory is drifting away
tell me for the 100th time
how good her dead husband John was
at pressing pants
*back in the day*
Joe steps out from behind his statue
of the Virgin Mary and waves
on his way to the wine shop

Bob crosses the street
with a book he had borrowed from me
and another he wants me to read
and a cigarette he shouldn't be smoking
because of his emphysema  my wife and daughter
are asleep inside   with no fear that bombs
will rip through our apartment walls and take them away
as they sleep   and I ask forgiveness
for this luxury  as the sun
un-shrouded and yet shrouded
by smoke  and the smell of death
breaks through the late summer leaves
somehow and yet again
everyday  everyday you

from THE SUM OF UNCOUNTABLE THINGS

**if things disappeared over the course of a day**. rather than over the stretch of a lifetime. this café where you are sitting right now. would already be dissolving. even when it seems like you have just gotten there. the barista would be there. lovely as she is one minute. and then simply gone the next. and you wouldn't have to get up and walk out wondering. what her sweet look meant. and if it did mean what it meant. was it meant just for you? because you will be dust. by the time this song. you haven't heard in ages. returns to the silence. from which it came. before you even have a chance to remember who sang it. once upon a time. and if the one whose neck you kissed long ago to this song. or one very much like it. still walks on this earth. or if that was just some yesterday. or what long ago passed as *yesterday*. before all the fast fading things of this world were made.

**there is no way to un-spell. what has been spelled by rain into our palms.** the word *dissolve* for instance. the way we learned to drive for example. I have ridden bicycles with movie reels for wheels. and ridden and ridden. until the films of everything I was riding toward jittered. on screens that were planted like billboards. along highways. between here and the next ocean. and still it's impossible to preempt our grieving. by imagining everything we love dissolving. like the rain in our palms. or the trees outside the windows when we first drove alone. dissolved. or the only photographs I had of her dissolved. not long after she herself dissolved. and *now* is only a word. like any other word. I would pronounce it. as if it has some special meaning. I would pronounce it now. if only.

**there is only one way to spell the word** *alibi*. despite your various misspellings of it. all these years. she wanted you to agree to call the lake where you first kissed her *alibi ocean*. but you couldn't. and that was the end of that. sometimes it seems like that game of holding your breath when you were a kid. or spinning until the world would spin with you. and keep spinning. after you had stopped spinning. the way every moment comes rushing back to you. at once. when a certain perfume mingles with bus fumes. or when pigeons explode into flight above a sidewalk. you used to carry a list of alibis around with you. in your wallet. alibis and a photograph of the palm reader who understood you. long after everyone else seemed to have stopped understanding you. maybe you would recognize that ocean now. the one that was only a lake. until it wasn't a lake anymore. if you were to suddenly come upon it. maybe you would reach for your phone. only to remember that you had finally taken her number out of your phone. after the rumor of her disappearance. became the fact of her dissolving. and spun and spun you. even after it seemed like the world had stopped spinning *what we owe* minus *what we own* **equals a sum greater or less than what matters after we have gone on**. multiplied of course by the number of birds that fly over the moment we are lowered back down into the earth. or by how many sparks fly up when our pyre ignites. divided naturally by the silence that comes after everyone has stopped speaking about us.

        please check your answers.
        please show all your work.

**in this photograph with a soundtrack by Ennio Morricone**
I have a six-shooter cap gun. and I'm shirtless and tan under a straw cowboy hat. leaning out around the corner of the house I lived in until I was eleven. my brothers are somewhere in the trees. their pistols trained on where they think I will reappear. the noon whistle blew hours ago.  and now cars are making their ways off the pike. and into our battlefield. all the moms are in the kitchens. rattling supper dishes like drums and cymbals. I stand still for a moment. trying to decide which tree I will run to for cover. a car door slams. and the percussion stops suddenly. someone's dad walks down a driveway. whistling. something I can almost hear. now. something coming from somewhere just on the other side of this world.  just on the other side of this. photograph.

**I dreamt I drove up to a house. many years before I was born.** and my mother came out. she held onto her hair. because of a sudden wind. she who was as beautiful as I remembered her from when I could first remember anything. *you're not born yet* she told me. *I know* I said *but I wanted to see you before all the letters of your alphabet started disappearing.* the wind was so loud in my dream. I'm not sure she heard me. *I will love you no matter what atrocities time commits* she shouted. *now drive away. drive away please.* she spoke and turned back. to a house I could not recognize. from any photograph. of any of the houses she had ever lived in. and I drove away. as she continued to walk through the wind. almost as if she were part of the wind herself. and I drove away. in a car I have never owned. and have only had the courage to drive in dreams.

**as far as I know. there is no such place. called** *the avalanche café*. there is no barista there. with dust on her lapels. no manager with the ash of who knows what. on his mustache. as far as I know. and as far as I know. there is no such place. with bleeding and bruised patrons. and tiny black coffees that must taste like nothing any of us has ever tasted. after a disaster such as this. after we had all become quite certain we would probably never taste coffee again. no such place exists. as far as I know. but if such a place does exist. the bell above the door just jingled. and there you are again. with the light of the outside world all around you. there you are. somehow even lovelier than I could have ever expected you to look. after all that has fallen. after all that keeps falling. upon us.

**sometimes we have shelves of photo albums.** walls lined with picture frames slideshows and home movies. teeming with evidence. of what or who we once were. and sometimes we don't even have an eyelash left anymore. to prove even to ourselves. that someone who is no longer. once wept onto our shoulder. or kissed and kissed our neck.

**whatever the sky is. the sky is blue**. in your memory. of the sky. and whatever the moon is. the moon is coming up. out of the ocean again. even if you are not there to watch the moon. come up out of the ocean again. whatever you are. you are undressing yourself. as you have undressed yourself. nearly every night before sleep. whether anyone remembers. how lovely you once were. undressing. how lovely you are now. undressing. whether anyone is there to tell you so. or simply to help you. with your buttons. this time.

*we slept like wine in forgotten bottles*. I said. about the way we used to sleep. once upon a time. we slept like electricity. in clipped wires. like birth control pills. in the medicine cabinets of vacant apartments. all the children who would neither be born nor not be born there. we slept like taxis after their drivers have crawled into bed. beside their sleeping wives. hoping perhaps for a little love. or at least to dream of something. other than traffic. we slept like the word *sleep* in a dictionary of a language nobody speaks anymore. in a library about to be bombed into rubble. just as the emptiness which was the library sleeps now that the library is gone. we slept like the severed tongues of those muted by decree centuries before we ever woke and slept and woke and slept again. we slept like wine in forgotten bottles. we slept like rivers sleep after they've spilled everything they are. or everything anyone thought they might one day become. into the huge mouth of the wide waking sea.

**the wrong turns I took. in the middle of your body**. in the middle of nowhere. in the middle of the night. the sirens or love moans I heard. from apartment windows. or from the reeds along the highways. of your body. the maps I thought I had. in my glove compartment. the glove compartment I thought I had. in my car. the car I thought I was driving. in the middle of nowhere. in the middle of the night. in the middle of your body. the wrong turns I took. and ended up somewhere. in a place I never expected. in a place I could not recognize. the wrong turns that took me. somewhere else. the sky there. the sea there. in the middle of your body. in the middle of nowhere. in the middle of the night

**at the end of all else let's remember**. the chef in Florence coming out of the kitchen. at the end of the night. with a guitar. and the drunk Scottish opera singer. doing his best *o solo mio*. let's never forget the owner throwing the *aperto* sign to *chiuso*. and the waitress dropping her apron to the floor. and stomping it away. as if it really did embody evil spirits. let's remember how we briefly danced then. as the windows steamed. how we ducked when the old woman upstairs banged her cane on her floor. and the ceiling thundered. as she threatened us with the wrath of the police. or worse. her dead husband. and his band of also-dead tough guys. and finally with Hell itself. to which she was singularly authorized to condemn us. before we and the chef and the opera singer and the waitress ran out into *oh my god Florence!* and disappeared into the alleyways. like the dust we once were. the dust we would one day become again. in the un-crowded museum of night.

**soon enough the highway will disappear**. and all the cars that have ever driven down  the highway. the songs we sang with the windows down will fade. into the greater hum of all gone noises. the dashboards. the windshields. the steering wheels. will be things nobody will remember. or mention ever again. and all that will be left then.  after everything else has dissolved. if we are lucky. will be the memory of your hand  briefly on top of mine. resting there on the gearshift. your fingers brushing my knuckles.  just before you lift them to your face. to tuck back that stray strand of hair. you always seemed to be tucking back. and the blur of trees out the window. and the flash of billboard out the window. will be all but begging us. to remember them too one day.  as if we will be here to do so. and if we are here.  as if we will have room left. in what's left of our memories. to remember anything else. at all.

**alibis pieced together from parade confetti. are not true alibis.** and alibis are never apologies. for what we couldn't help ourselves from doing. just as an alarm clock is not a getaway car. every day she gets a little taller than the ocean. and yet she stands next to the ocean and feels tiny. I was sleeping when I was accused of being awake. but that is not my alibi. yes I put my ear to your chest. when you were dreaming. yes I listened for the bird-bone clicks that would open your safe. yes I wanted to step into the vault of you. into the place where you keep the most precious pieces of yourself. but all I could hear was your breathing. fast and short. as if you were running away from someone or some thing chasing you. and then I took my safe-cracking tools. and buried them behind the barn. with the loot we would never spend. as I said before. or sort of said. *a getaway car is not an alarm clock*. your honor. once I was just a little boy.

**I don't know how I got here. at this. the only café left. at the end of the world.** I can't remember what wrong turn. led me down one street. that turned into another and then into this alley. that dead-ends here at this seat. but here I am. with no cellphone signal. and my watch seems to have stopped. the waitress speaks no language I have ever heard. in my brief stint among languages. she has the smoothest skin and the greenest eyes I have ever seen. I did not even ask and she brought me the most beautiful black coffee. in the tiniest white cup. and that's when I realized. suddenly.  sadly. and with a little relief. I must admit.  that this must be how it ends.

IN WHICH WE ALL KISS SOMETHING SECRETLY

in which the dogs of vacant lots were barking at empty freight trains in which the city you once knew could still be seen from the balcony in which the harbor lights lit your kitchen at 3AM in which the polished chrome of the butcher shop reflected your face in which the barista was a world-class musician pulling coffees to pay child support in which blood stained the cannibals' bibs in which the text messages of young lovers were all erased with one lightning strike in which towns are named for automobiles and children are named after towns in which the ragged map looked like entrails spilling out of the glove compartment in which the distance between her breasts and her thighs seemed like a lifetime in which the gas station attendant is your father forty years ago without the pain of years in his eyes in which there were flowers outside the fire house for years after the explosion in which one restaurateur is dragged away by the police from the bedroom of another restaurateur in which she quoted whole passages of things you told her years ago in which a screaming girl ran through the train car and you recognized her from another dream in which the only way to describe the stillness is to say *the bridges are holding their breath* in which the millionaire folds other people's laundry on Henry Street in which the shoe repairman dreamt of being a longshoreman who dreamed of being a wiseguy in which the silence between oceans was lit by all night diners in which her misspelled name was stitched to her uniform in which you rode on my shoulders until I went back down into the earth in which *afternoon* was renamed *beforedusk* in which Venice was no longer underwater in which a piano dangled above the sidewalk café from a hangman's noose in which we blinked and the moment was gone and we too in which the authorities exclaim their astonishment and then quickly calm themselves in which the downstairs neighbor is a genius not an idiot banging on the ceiling at every noise in which the sad automobiles of rush hour are hardly rushing at all in which you loved me as if there were nothing else and no time left in which the magazine cover photos were of factory workers and traffic cops in which the day's limp to the horizon was like the broken gallop of a long-ago horse in which the women dried themselves with towels the color of vanilla and sage in which the Himalayas were skyscrapers and the Sahara was a vacant lot in which I came in empty-handed and left empty-handed in which our memories try to become alibis for any accusations that come our way in which there were birds the drab of coffee grounds in which the sky was the pale gray of an emptied ashtray in which my mother was behind the wheel of the Pontiac and my father was on the lawn with a garden hose in which the woman at the café asked the silence *is there no place for me in this angry world?*

in which the mugshot was clearly of a scarecrow but not even the victim of the crime could see that in which there was your body and my body and the ache between our bodies in which the word *dissolving* was written in the sky by birds' wings  in which you tried to take the clouds you fell through with you into your dying in which there is no one on the sidewalk and it is raining in which you touch me and remember what it was like to pretend to be blind in which you had many secrets and  forgot they were secrets and then forgot they ever happened at all in which afternoon is a wound opening in the day's torso in which the landscape is a yellow blur from the window of a train in which silence is neither a word nor the absence of a word in which we met anonymously in some anonymous dusk in which *all at once is what eternity is* in which I am not Kenneth Patchen but then again neither was Kenneth Patchen in which this is a dream and you are the one having this dream in which we arrived at the appointed time said the prescribed things and left when we were supposed to leave in which the dead of your life are sitting around the table talking about you as if you were the one who had died in which the sky above the city is the only one of us left who remembers our kisses in which the exit sign is not in the photograph but the photograph is called *the exit sign* in which we were in our bathing suits and our bicycles were against the fence and the sky was so blue we would never be able to unforget it in which the concierge at *hotel amnesia* takes your coat and then asks you for your coat in which the telegram was addressed to *Monsieur November* but the bellboy read it to you anyway in which you wish you were transparent and indistinguishable from the air in which fingertips are whispers and your whispers are the only evidence that you undid my belt buckle and that we committed the crime of once knowing each other at all in which the highway ends one chapter and begins the next in which you are in an uncertain place and yet the place you are going is even more uncertain in which this is the soundtrack called *in which* in which the ocean's autobiography is called *in lieu of flowers* in which the arsonist is in love with a girl he refers to as *electricity* in which *your honor once I was just a little boy* is no longer an admissible plea of not guilty in which the only way to describe the sun is with the made-up adjective *effiginous* in which there was a museum and an afternoon in a museum and now that museum and that afternoon are gone  in which one of them died screaming and the other fell asleep and never woke up  in which the sky is ransacked every five o'clock by ransacking birds  in which *sorry for your loss* is how the arsonist greets his wife every morning  in which we were on a train and I was watching her and she was young and I was  young and now she is no longer and I am no longer young in which the scarecrow wishes he were an effigy and the effigy wants to be a piñata and the piñata is longing to one day be the moon and the moon has a wish list of who she'd rather be that would stretch from here to the moon in which the arsonist that is your heart is setting fires all over again in which you have broken bread with murderers without acknowledging that they were murderers because they were so well-spoken and because they laughed at your jokes in which you were running away from something in your dream but never left your desk chair the whole time you were awake in which Maestro Ennio Morricone is contemplating a length of string and the hills are yellow under the blue sky out his window in which you are quite certain that you could make yourself disappear if it weren't for how much you would miss certain people in which you walk all over the city and always end up at the same restaurant and sit in the same chair and order the same thing – summer rolls and hollow vegetables with garlic sauce and a Vietnamese beer  in which a woman is crossing and re-crossing her legs in time to the stoplight outside the window and nobody seems to notice and nobody calls it a *phenomenon* in which a piano in an upstairs window when it's raining is enough to make you remember the taste of kisses in which *breathe* is on your to-do list in which she took off her glasses and looked up from her book and finally you submitted to amnesia in which the elephants that walked across the Brooklyn Bridge to show the skeptical and the scared that the bridge could hold their weight had no idea that they would appear a hundred years later in dreams about things falling.

in which you are homesick for a time when it was still possible to get lost in which if we have learned anything we haven't learned it from this phrasebook in which there were horses running through the sunlight as if we didn't have a choice to not believe in beauty in which you were dreaming of things falling and when you woke up there were things falling in which a man who looked like he slept in an ashtray paced back and forth on the corner with a smoking briefcase laughing and shaking his head and then put the briefcase down and walked away while it drizzled confetti even though there was no parade in which there was a cellist at your breakfast table and she was lovely and you were twenty-one and you have no idea what ever happened to her in which you were sleeping and then you woke up and there was suddenly Chicago through the windshield in which your father was dying and decided to fall out of an airplane and you were certain that he would do something to make sure that his chute didn't open but it did and he stood up and started telling jokes all over again as if he hadn't just fallen through the clouds in which you swim and you swim and you swim and you still don't know if you really know how to swim in which a line of people is walking toward the horizon and some people are joining the line without knowing why and one of them says *even if we get to that horizon there will be another one farther out what then?* in which you had been making out for so long in someone's basement that your tongue hurt and you thought your jeans might be worn smooth at the crotch in which the conductor of this train dreams of becoming an astronaut and is quite sure that his wife is having an affair with his sister in which the ocean is always the ocean even if we act as if there is no ocean out there in which there is an abandoned house just off the highway and there is a windmill next to the house and after you climb over the barbed-wire fence and walk around the cow patties and step then through what was once the front door of that house you announce *honey I'm home* and you feel like you are indeed home perhaps for the first time in a very long time in which there are dishwashers dreaming of becoming poets and poets washing last night's dishes and the same cardinal is outside both of their windows in the morning singing *am I alive am I alive am I alive?* in which here continues the long slow lesson of loneliness in which sometimes the body is surrounded by thousands of tiny moths in which the trouble with horses is the same trouble with revenge and this has something to do with the sudden eruption of stillness into stampede in which we give names to fragrances as if we can give names to fragrances in which you own five of the same shirt and five of the same pair of pants and one hat and you are trying to find a store that sells it so you can buy four more in which sometimes the body is held by another body and sometimes the body sleeps next to another body but in which the body always seems to be alone nevertheless  in which you never understood architecture until you suddenly understood architecture in which the drummer closed his eyes and tried to recreate the color of 1974 and his father's car pulling into the driveway  in which we have never danced together except that one time we danced together but that was just in your dream which you now regret telling me about in which we always remember the phone booths where we learned things we wished we never learned and never quite remember which ocean it was where we forgot them again in which it's the birds that are holding up the sky and not the other way around in which I had wings but hadn't told you yet and you had wings but hadn't discovered it yet in which the body isn't an outline on a sidewalk but knows it will be one day soon in which Ennio Morricone is sitting in the barber's chair and a Sergio Leone movie is playing on the television in the corner and the barber is whistling along but has no idea whose hair he is cutting in which nothing is more beautiful than the loneliness of the getaway driver after the robbery is botched and he's still sitting on the curb watching the police lights and deciding when to slowly pull away from the curb in which the body sometimes has its own light and somehow this is related to stars in which the mirror shows only your defeats and none of your victories in which sometimes the body is the body and sometimes it is not anything with a life of its own at all in which the moon dissolves like a lozenge in the smoky mouth of night in which *dissolve* is the only verb left that you use when speaking of yourself in which you rode a bus through Ohio and the woman next to you in a leg cast and a neck brace fell asleep on your shoulder and kissed your neck in the night in which the pilot says *ladies and gentlemen we are experiencing some turbulence* and the man next to you says under his breath *welcome to the club* in which the father came home from the war and winced whenever anything fell or was spilled in which the neighbor cut his small lawn with a pair of scissors every day and tended a cactus garden of all things in Pennsylvania of all places in which there is nothing like the loneliness of seeing your mother's cigarette glow on the porch from a block away and think *that's how I can tell where home is* in which I am writing to you now from an undisclosed location and will ask the cleaning lady to have her sister take my letter with her back to Honduras and drop it in the mail from there in which the schoolgirl is in love with the soccer player and mentions him first and last in her prayers every night in which we ran through the yards after throwing tomatoes at the city buses and dogs were barking and men in t-shirts were smoking at kitchen tables in which there was a bullet hole in the bathroom sink at your best friend's house and nobody ever talked about it in which you wonder how many of your students have touched themselves while thinking about you in which you have touched yourself trying not to think of your students in which the moon appears like a lozenge on the tongue of the horizon in which Federico Fellini owns the pizzeria next to the barber shop and the barber is you are quite certain Nino Rota in which Joseph Cornell is your accountant and you have to convince your memory that your mother is not Anna Magnani in which the moon breaks in two like a lozenge when you bite down too hard on the night in which the trumpeter at the end of the train platform doesn't know you but is playing your childhood as if he invented it himself in which the daylight and all the things of the daylight ambush you where you lie and in which the night ransacks what's left of your heart in which the moon's attempted apologies for what the sun did only end up sounding like excuses in which there was a bicycle on her lawn and she came out of the house and said *kiss me* and you kissed her and someone stole the bicycle and you both took off running down the street screaming and laughing in which the birds that fly out of the piñata are the same birds you swear flew out of the magician's fist in a different dream in which it is Easter and all the bells in Paris are ringing and you are running back to your apartment to be there when your parents call and you tell them you were out listening to the bells and not lying next to a woman who would not let you touch her in which August breaks us into pieces and September says *it's not my problem* in which the debutante's wedding dress is stained with vomit and the boot prints of those she invited to undress her in which you went to Spain and said *now I can never again say I've never been to Spain* in which *yellow* is the color of the hills in your dream and the sky is so blue you cannot describe it to anyone who has not had the same dream in which you swear you hear sirens and screams when the refrigerator motor kicks on in which it's 1960 and your parents are not your parents yet but they are in love and watching Louis Armstrong sweating in a Navy club in which any one of us could be the first taken should the greater intelligence who possibly set this simulation called *us* into motion decides the game is over  in which a man dressed as a janitor steps onto a train and announces the next act which he says will blow our minds and then stands back while nothing happens at all in which the fragments of all your dreams converge into one long dream in which you are broken and lonely and sitting on a bench hoping that nobody notices and hoping that somebody notices  in which the streets are deserts and the people walking down the streets are mirages  in which a woman who tries but fails to set herself on fire and then tries but fails to jump off a bridge is contemplating not killing herself anymore in which a violist is listening to the slowed-down recording of bees and feeling like she is hearing music for the first time.

in which you are terrified of fires and there are fires in which you are terrified of melting ice and there is melting ice in which the trains are stopped in the tunnels and you are terrified of trains stopped in tunnels in which the elevator doors won't open and you are terrified you are terrified and you are terrified of being terrified in which the worst among us have taken the wheel and we are in the backseat just trying to watch the landscape before it disappears just trying to hold each other's hand before each other's hand disappears and we are terrified of the worst among us and they are at the wheel and their feet are on the pedals and they are telling us that they are the best among us and you are terrified of the worst among us in which the ventriloquist doesn't know what to make his dummy say in which the ballerina cannot remember how to dance in which the mariachi band forgets that it is all ending and plays on into the darkest of the dark and you are not terrified for a moment of the dark in which you suddenly remember you are terrified of the dark and you are terrified by suddenly remembering in which you have forgotten everything else except how terrified you are and you are terrified of forgetting everything else in which houses and highways and parking lots and shopping plazas are being eaten by fire and you are terrified of being eaten by fire in which water is rising and you are terrified in which temperatures are rising and you are terrified in which your city is sinking and you are terrified of your city sinking and you are terrified of water rising and you are terrified that the worst among us are not terrified in which the worst among us are on the TV are waving at the cameras are joking about the air we are supposed to be breathing and you are terrified in which the best among us are terrified and you are terrified in which you are most terrified that the best among us are terrified

ENNIO MORRICONE IS DISSOLVING

## Ennio Morricone is Not Ennio Morricone

Ennio Morricone if you ask Ennio Morricone is not Ennio Morricone   he is not the man at the barber shop telling the barber to go a little shorter on the sides this time   he is not thinking *I have to be in New York and then I have to be in London and I don't want to have to go to a barber in either place*   he is not the man walking down *via della madonna dell'Orto* with a newspaper under his arm  with freshly-shined shoes   with a watch that he had just had fixed   he is not Ennio Morricone


Ennio Morricone is not the man in front of Pasticceria Valzani seeing the reflection of Ennio Morricone in the glass   Ennio Morricone is not the man sitting now at a caffè with his newspaper on his lap   with scribblings of notes and rests between notes on his napkin   next to his saucer   an embouchure of coffee on the lip of his cup

Ennio Morricone is not Ennio Morricone anymore than you or I am Ennio Morricone


except when he rises right now from his table and tries to get his ears above the snare brush and timpani of the streets   to hear what he thought at first was a siren but then realized was a bird   that anyone might mistake for a siren   Ennio Morricone rising from his seat becomes Ennio Morricone for a moment and he holds that moment his ears trying to find that bird his ears running through the streets to find it and then he sits again and tries to remember when he was that man tries to remember when he  Ennio Morricone was Ennio Morricone  just a moment ago rising in order to become Ennio Morricone

in order to become Ennio Morricone   Ennio Morricone needs to first dress like a gentleman  always a jacket usually a tie  pressed pants  leather shoes   Ennio Morricone needs to have his hair cut every Monday   in order to become Ennio Morricone  he needs to sit at the same seat at the same table at the same caffè at the same time every day   except Sunday  and take his espresso   after a glass  of sparkling water   while staring straight ahead  in order to become Ennio Morricone  in order to become Ennio Morricone   Ennio Morricone needs to rise from the same seat at the same table at the same caffè at the same time   precisely 23 minutes after sitting down  and count out the change in his palm  and place it just so on his receipt  and take his jacket from the back of the chair and put it on if it is cool   and fold it neatly over his forearm if it is warm  and brush any crumbs  though  he knows there are no crumbs off his pants and then nod to the waiter in the doorway  and step out onto the sidewalk and place his hat on his head   and look at the sun over the buildings across the street  and walk  as calmly as he walked here  then in order to become Ennio Morricone  Ennio Morricone must walk down the sidewalk in no apparent hurry   and with no apparent urgency to anyone else but Ennio Morricone  because in order to become Ennio Morricone  Ennio Morricone must be bursting now with the theme for the end of the film  he is scoring   and in order to become Ennio Morricone   Ennio Morricone must not let anyone know that these notes are about to explode out of him as soon as he returns to his apartment  as soon as he sits down again at his piano  in order to become Ennio Morricone  Ennio Morricone must keep this secret  down one street and across the next  past the old man sitting in his chair outside his building  the old woman sweeping the stairs  Ennio Morricone must never let them know that he is anything other than a man of precise routines  a man bothered only by what bothers us  concerned about only what we are concerned about  and finally in order to become Ennio Morricone  Ennio Morricone must sit at his piano  and exhale and inhale and exhale again and then say to himself  *I have done what I have needed to do to become Ennio Morricone and now I am*

sometimes Ennio Morricone

sometimes Ennio Morricone closes his eyes and imagines moments from some of his favorite scenes he has composed music for and wishes that he could remember what they were like without his music underneath them when they were simply light and movement and image

sometimes Ennio Morricone wishes he could bend at the waist or better yet drop to a knee before these scenes and look them straight in the eye and ask them to tell him everything again like children who haven't yet learned how to speak.

in which Ennio Morricone is flying over the ocean

in which Ennio Morricone is flying over the ocean  in which the woman next to him says she is Kashmiri  in which she sings a few bars of a song to Ennio Morricone in Persian  in which Ennio Morricone then falls asleep while flying over the ocean with the Persian song in his head and the warmth of the Kashmiri woman next to him  in which back in Rome in Fiumicino Airport the woman is swept up into the hugs and tears of the family waiting for her and Ennio Morricone waves back to her when she waves  in which Ennio Morricone says *Fiumicino little river* to himself a few times and then starts singing it while he is waiting for his luggage  *Fiumicino Fiumicino little river Fiumicino*  to the tune of the Persian song the woman sang to him while flying over the ocean  in which this little song becomes a trumpet interlude in a soundtrack Ennio Morricone composes later for a movie with Monica Vitti in it  in which Ennio Morricone watches that movie later at a cinema festival and hears that trumpet interlude and remembers Fiumicino and that Persian woman and her little song in his ear while he was flying over the ocean  in which Ennio Morricone takes his wife's hand at the movie when Monica Vitti is looking off as the trumpet interlude fades as if to say *yes she is beautiful but this music is about you*  in which Ennio Morricone is saying  *it has always been about you Fiumicino little river it has always been about you*

## Ennio Morricone is Dissolving

Ennio Morricone is dissolving in a field of sunflowers. he is wearing a well-tailored suit and heavy-rimmed glasses. his hair is slicked back. let's call this moment *studio numero cento*. or let's call it *study in dissolving*. let's pretend that those mosquitoes are far-off violins. let's imagine that the breeze-rattling of sunflower stalks is the far-off approach of percussion. just as Ennio Morricone would have wanted it. you might think this is 1974 or 1967. if it weren't for the fact that Ennio Morricone looks much older now in whatever year this is than he did back then. from the photographs you have seen of him from back then. and yet he looks as if he might have been standing here for centuries. the sunflowers grow up. they turn their heads toward the sun. *girasole* you remember from your Italian book. *gira*-ing toward the *sole*. they droop their heads and then they fall. and Ennio Morricone is dissolving. as if he were any of a number of *spaventapasseri*. any of a number of scarecrows. dissolving. as new crops of *girasole* grow up again from the seeds their ancestors have dropped. and the sun sets and rises. sets and rises. Ennio Morricone is dissolving. and somehow holding himself as still as a daguerreotype. as if any sudden movement might cause him to shatter like glass. to burst open. and spill all his dreams. like seeds. the glass seeds. of Ennio Morricone's dreams. scattering everywhere. onto the ground and into the wind. as if they weren't even his dreams to have. as if he weren't even here to dream them.

as the credits rolled

at the end of this movie I dreamt in which I was a bicyclist in the Wild West and you were the pretty girl with a fast gun the sunset was the color of smoked salmon and the mountains looked like paintings of mountains I said *if I'm really the hero I should ride this here bicycle into that sunset* and you said *what bicycle?* and shot it out from under me with your lightning-fast six-shooter and I said *I reckon I could walk* and I started walkin' and you caught up to me holstering your smoking gun while Ennio Morricone himself sauntered out from the green room behind the mountains humming a song so longing so beautiful we couldn't help wishing that this was our forever this sun this music and those ushers down there dragging their trashbags silently through the aisles.

LINER NOTES (*ASH* – MAT MANERI QUARTET)

I built on the sand
And it tumbled down,
I built on a rock
And it tumbled down.
Now when I build, I shall begin
With the smoke from the chimney.


Leopold Staff, translated from the Polish by Czeslaw Milosz
(written immediately after WWII)

## Ash

in which a man covered in ash leaves his briefcase also covered in ash on the sidewalk and walks away from it on the sidewalk and the briefcase remains on the sidewalk for days until it falls over ashes spilling out of it and birds descend upon it and rain descends upon it and ash runs like ink into the gutter and then the briefcase is gone and all that's left on the sidewalk are faint outlines of what was once something before it was  ash

in which ash is not a prerequisite but is not ash without prerequisites what has burned  what is still burning  in order for there to be ash

in which it seems only the phoenix rises from ash  ash's single moment of preceding something  anything  other than what is washed away after ash is washed away

in which ash has a walk-on part as a prerequisite to flight

in which at this very moment they are digging for survivors if there are any survivors through ash and then they will be digging for those who didn't survive  and there will be those who didn't survive  in the ash in which  we knew when to come home from where we played on the empty lot when it was dark enough to see our mother's cigarette glowing through its ash where she sat on the porch

in which the word for *ash* in so my languages sounds like what you would imagine ash might sound like if you could hear the sound ash makes when it lands – *asshe, æsċe, askā, askō̜, asshe, ashe, aska, aske, etc. etcetera*

in which the many words for *ash* almost sound like *etcetera*

the etcetera of ash

dust to dust

in which dust itself is a prerequisite for dust   in which dust is in a mote of dust in which dust is in a float of dust  afloat as a mote of dust in which dust as a speck

in which a speck of dust is flicked off a lapel   flicked off a lapel and landing somewhere else   in which the same dust speck is back later only we don't recognize it as such   in which dust is kicked up from leaving one place to go to another

in which there is a dust up   a light dusting   in which the dust settles   in which someone maybe you or I are left in the dust

in which in the blues song *dust my broom* means *leave this place forever*

and that song is composed of *floating verses*

in which dust is the only thing moving when nothing else is moving

in which dust is the aftermath of skin   the aftermath of hair   the floating away of pollen

in which dust announces itself in a slice of sunlight

in which when nothing else is moving dust is moving

in which dust lands  with sound that must be like the sound of ash landing if we only have the ability to hear it

in which dust returns to dust and again and again dust to dust and then dust to dust again as if there is no end

in which there is no end except in the repeating of the end

Earth

in which the word *earth* all by itself is now a lament for what once seemed like it could never end

in which the word *earth* itself is now a longing  a nostalgia a trying a trying a trying to grab the reins even though the horses know exactly where they are going and the reins are out of reach

in which the dust of earth  the ash of earth  the dust of the ash  the ash of the dust of earth

in which it's possible to hold a speck of dust  a cinder of ash in your hand and say *this was once the earth*

in which what have we done? what have we allowed to be done? what do we leave  after we leave what we have done?

in which the word *earth* and the etcetera of what we have done to the earth and

## Brahms

in which Brahms wrote to his last love Agathe von Siebold, *I am incapable of bearing fetters.* and then that he wanted to *clasp* her in his arms

in which this music cannot bear fetters and yet clasps its memories tight

in which Tennessee Williams has Carol Cutrere in *Orpheus Descending* say: *what on earth can you do but catch at whatever comes near you with both your hands until your fingers are broken* ...

in which this melody comes back like dust   like ash   like dust

in which returning to a melody from one's past is like stepping into a room and the memory of that room can be simply nostalgia or it can rise from its own ashes and find flight

in which Orpheus in which Carol Cutrere in which Brahms in which the fetters are unable to be borne and yet the desire to clasp what we can clasp in our hands until our fingers are broken is always there

in which

Glimmer

in which there are glimmers

in which hope

in which my daughter when she was three thought Thelonious Monk was *the loneliest monk*

in which it's there  Monk is there  as Brahms was there before Monk was there  and both are still there  because of hope because of glimmers of hope  because of the fifth player in every quartet is a ghost

in which the fifth player in this quartet is actually not a ghost but the act of listening to ghosts and to each other

in which nobody quite listens like this  listens not just with the ears but with everything that came before and everything that came after and everything that is coming now through the ether

in which it's there because if you listen to the ether you can hear what is there inside the noise of the silence of the ether

in which what is inside the noise of the silence of the ether can only be caught like ash  like dust like a glimmer  if any of any of that can be caught at all

## Moon

in which there was no moon and then there was a moon as slender as a glimpse   as slender as a keyhole   as slender as an eyelash

in which there was a glimmer of it and then there was the moon but then it too was gone

in which it too and its glimmer were gone

in which orbit  in which phases  in which lovers pause and look up

in which the moon holds its breath hoping you don't notice that she is dissolving   that she is made not of light but of ash   of dust   of wishes

in which the lament of its suspension there

in which the lament of the lament of its suspension there

## Cold World Lullaby

in which even if you don't know the references  you know the references

in which you can see the spy who lived in the pages of a book and then lived on a movie screen  in which you can see him and then

in which you hear the lament of *lume lume  earth earth* the lament of what comes from the earth and then what goes back to the earth what rots there so there is room for another to be here

in which you can hear it even if you don't know the references  even if you don't know the tune  you are singing it too  *lume lume  earth earth*

in which the tears of the woman are the tears pulled from the strings

in which the tears are for this earth as is the earth the soil that which takes our dust that which takes our ash

but in which the tears are also for this Earth  its slow orbit  even after we have dusted our brooms

and in which the lullaby to the cold world  or the cold world is singing the lullaby and then another lullaby comes   pulled from the deeper strings   in another tongue  an unidentifiable lullaby  in a different tongue

in which it comes on deeper strings   this lullaby   once sung by a grandfather to a boy  so it has to now be on deeper strings

in which it returns now  as we return *lume lume* as if it's possible to come in from the cold

in which the earth is asleep  asleep now

IT'S NOT THE OLYMPICS

It's not the olympics

it's not the olympics
it's not the election
it's people burning
alive while praying

it's not the new series you're binging
it's not the coffee you discovered
from Ethiopia
it's not the new boyfriend of the pop singer

it's children burning
alive while praying

it's not how much you saved
on your mortgage
what you pay for your car lease
how long it takes you
to get to work

it's mother and fathers
and grandmothers
and grandfathers
burning alive while praying

it's not how many home runs
the home run hero has
who's in first in the Eastern Division
how much they pay the new forward

it's the bombs
that came out of the early morning sky
and then the people burning
alive while praying

it's not the fascist candidate's
new nickname for the non-fascist candidate
who is much better
than the fascist candidate
but won't really do anything to stop this
no matter how much we hope
she'll do something  anything
to stop this

it's not  how likable or unlikeable
their running mates are

it's people bathing themselves
and laying out their prayer mats
and lowering themselves
to send their prayers to the sky
and that same sky
raining down on them
with bombs
that burn them alive
while praying

it's not your retirement account
or maybe it is your retirement account
it's not your IRA
or maybe it is your IRA
it's not the interest you earned
or maybe it is the interest you earned

it's not the rhetoric of the people who drop the bombs
or the rhetoric of the people
the people they say they are dropping the bombs on
it's the people who aren't those people at all
burning alive while praying

it's not your new shoes
or your new haircut
or your new way of sleeping
it's not your new pickleball paddle
or your new drum sticks
it's not your shiny new car
in your newly paved driveway
with your freshly cut grass
and the fact that you spray
less harsh chemicals on your lawn
than you used to
since you watched that instagram video
about what those chemicals
you used to spray
do to the river
and the people who live downriver
and now you feel better
about the less harsh chemicals
you spray on your lawn
it's not the scent you smelled on
someone else's neck
and asked what it was
and then forgot
as soon as you walked away
only to smell it again

dozens of times
each time
almost remembering its name
only to find yourself googling it
trying to discover it
despite everything else
that came up
on your computer screen

it's people
people
kneeling down
after washing
after laying out their prayer mats
kneeling down
to pray
in what they thought was a safe place
because the government that bombed them
told them it was a safe place
and then hearing the aircraft
before they were able to go anywhere
and where could they go
there was no place else to go
and the government that bombed them
also cut off the water supply

to where they are now praying
to the place where they were told
they would be safe where they could shelter
and they woke up in the early morning hours
to pray to be safe enough to pray
and they heard the aircraft
and they looked into the sky
they were praying toward
and before they knew it
the bombs tore through the school
it's not how outraged you are
for a few minutes
when you watch the coverage
you can barely watch
and then for a few minutes after
it's not how quickly you get over
your outrage
when that new series is queued up
and you open a new bottle of wine
or take your gummy
or mix that new mocktail
that helps you go to sleep
it's not how much you like
your new whitening toothpaste
your new eye pillow

your new way of sleeping
with your face in the breeze
of the air cleaner
it's not the email you forgot
to send
or the text you just can't read right now
or the message you plan to write
tomorrow that will
you hope end the dispute
at your job
it's people it's children it's mothers
it's fathers it's grandmothers
it's grandfathers it's people
brothers sisters uncles aunts
parents and children it's people
it's not your discomfort
at thinking this
at having to think about this
of being asked to think about this
of wishing you didn't have to be
thinking about this

it's people
people burning
people burning alive

it's people burning alive
while praying.

IF WE ARE NOT MIRAGES

if we are not mirages

what business do we have

disappearing

just as we seem to be

coming into view

## if we are not mirages

despite night's fist on the scruff of your neck you try to sleep   there are highways out there that end themselves unceremoniously under overpasses  or just after road signs announce that they will end  and the country roads they become  slow at blinking yellow lights  at intersections in towns  where you'll never walk   where you'll never fall in love  and someone in one of those windows in one of those towns is at a table with photographs weeping  and someone has just walked across the room in another one of those towns and locked a cat in a bathroom you will never know that cat but you can hear her howling when the radiator in the hall stops banging  or is it not the cat but the squeak of the box lid when the weeping person closes up the photographs perhaps for the last time ever   you are in one of those photographs you realize what's the chance of that?  there you are  in a crowd at a tourist site you can hardly recognize yourself now  but it has to be you with people who aren't even alive now buying you ice cream  and pointing at things you are supposed to see  and the person  who has closed the box didn't know you then or now especially now that the box is closed   perhaps forever   the woman with the cat is up again  she opens the door and sits by the window the cat jumps into her lap  there they are above the intersection of one road  with another road that was a country road that was a highway before that  there they are in the yellow when the light blinks on  and there they aren't a moment later when the light blinks off there they are  and then there they aren't   there and then not there again what business do we have

for a while the years were like bullets trying to put themselves back into a gun  now they are scattered around on the floor like pieces of a puzzle  that is either of a starless night sky  or of Kazimir Malevich's painting *Black Square*  I can't tell which  and the box went out the door with the trash ages ago  last night I woke up at 3 AM with the sudden realization that there were ghosts in the room  one was my mother asking me if I would sit with her when the next rain comes  the other was my brother telling me how much he doesn't regret not growing old  the geese on the pond had gone silent  there were no other sounds except my breathing  *this is not my bed* I thought  *not my house  that is not my pond  the silence of the geese is not mine  nor will their explosion of chattering an hour or so from now be mine  all that is mine is my breath right now and my breath is just on loan  until I can't use it anymore*  the ghosts come in and out of the room  or is it the cat  I don't know  regardless  I breath them in  I breathe them out.

## disappearing

there are rest stops in our road trips between one sleep and the next  you see one up ahead and calculate the lanes you need to cross to pull off the highway  to slow gradually  to not have to brake hard and not disrupt the other passengers if anyone is with you or more likely the papers on the dash the groceries on the backseat if you're alone  and you are most likely alone  ideally you'll pull in  take the correct lane for parking and park  and rest  there is no need to get out and step into the garish marketplace of urinating and sunglasses of fried everything and vibrating chairs  perhaps you should at least step out though and stretch  perhaps you should walk to where a spit of trees and grass approximates nature  you'll have to ignore the teenagers  vaping and groping on a picnic table that wasn't put there for such things  but has served that purpose  more than any other since it was put there  and you'll kick your shoes off even though you know thousands of dogs have pissed there and feel your toes come close to the earth  or perhaps you'll just sit there with the steering wheel not knowing what to do with itself without your hands on it  staring out at the drivers and passengers adjusting their underwear as they come back to their cars  perhaps you'll not judge them  this time  as you wouldn't want to be judged next time or perhaps not  perhaps you won't even notice them and simply feel what it feels like not to be moving so fast down the highway to simply feel what it feels like to take this moment as you don't take enough moments to not be counting mile markers or minutes   and to just breathe just as we seem to be

in lieu of *no matter how fleeting* please send a forever that cannot be overthrown

in lieu of *this moment* please send an unexpected memory of this moment

in lieu of *last night's moon* please send another moon tonight

in lieu of *a dice cup's spill of stars* please send a fist rattle of the same stars

in lieu of *this ocean* please send any body of water impersonating this ocean

coming into view

if we are not mirages

what business do we have

disappearing

just as we seem to be

coming into view

# acknowledgments

For their contributions to the space for making, the making itself, the publishing and the exhibiting, and for the proliferation of the work in this collection, I'd like to thank (in somewhat chronological order): Rhonda Keyser, Chris Coates, Greg Hershey, Eddie Williams, Ron Bayes (RIP), Mark Nowak, Theodore Enslin (RIP), John Taggart, Elena Alexander, Agha Shahid Ali (RIP), Michael Carroll, Edmund White, Don Matteson, Cedric N. Chatterley, Antonio Migliaccio, Patrick Ryan, The New York Foundation for the Arts, Patricia Watkins, Luquer Street Press, Hyatt Bass, Josh Klausner, Maybelle Keyser-Butson, Joseph AW Quintela, Stephen Lipuma, Amy Ng, Maria Mercedes Martinez, Maria Saha, Karen Revis, Orazio de Gennaro, Walter Rossi, Melissa Goodling, Gary Butson, Eric Maierson, Dennis Dawson, Toni Ann Serratelli, Lorraine Doran, Zoë Ryder White, Mat Maneri, BACAS (Teggiano, Italy), Barbès Brooklyn, Terence Degnan, City of Asylum (Pittsburgh), Zachary Lazar, Tulane University, The Italian Cultural Institute of Chicago, four one one (Brooklyn), Hungry Brain (Chicago), Jazz Gallery (Milwaukee), Trinosophes (Detroit), Nublu (New York), Marc Urselli, East Side Studios, At Home on Hudson (Kingston), and PEN GEORGIA/The 9th Annual Tbilisi International Festival of Literature.

and to Eliot Cardinaux and The Bodily Press for believing that these poems also exist on the page with or without the music.

Most importantly, I would like to thank the musicians who have inspired me, not only with their musicianship and enthusiasm for this work and for collaborating with me on it, but also with their intense sensitivity and listening which takes me as a poet and these poems to places I didn't think possible: Dave Park, Mat Maneri, Marco Cappelli, Damon Banks, Dave Miller, Lucian Ban, Avram Fefer, Brandon Lopez, Randy Peterson, Jordan Perry, JT Lewis, and Marc Ribot.

# Notes

I wrote ***repeat after me*** as a response to the "blood drawings" of Pietro Costa, inspired by the repetition of the square and the repetition of the minimal content within the square. The poem, along with his drawings, received a New York Foundation for the Arts Fellowship for "Artist Books" in 2003. I first began performing these poems and variations on them with violist Mat Maneri in 2004 in Brooklyn, and have performed them many times over the years with him, and most recently with the addition of pianist Lucian Ban, in New Orleans and Kingston, New York.

Originally conceived in the early 1990s, in response to a friend's insistence that I had too many crows in my poems, ***let's move all things*** *(when the crow is removed)* began as a series of poems in which I took any poem of mine that had the word crow or any reference to a crow in it and removed that and using only the other words created a new poem. The series has evolved into variations on lines within the poem and has been a poem I have returned to for almost thirty years. I first performed this poem with bassist Dave Park in Richmond, Virginia and then in New York, and have recently performed fragments of it again in Brooklyn with guitarists Marco Cappelli and Marc Ribot and drummer JT Lewis, and in Tbilisi, Georgia with saxophonist Rezo Kiknadze.

Visual Artist Maria Mercedes Martinez and I collaborated in 2019 on a series of assemblages (handmade light boxes with her snapshots and my poems). This project, ***in which we all kiss something secretly***, premiered at Court Tree Collective Gallery in Brooklyn that year, with a chapbook of the same name published simultaneously. On the opening night of the exhibition, Mat Maneri and guitarist Marco Cappelli accompanied me as we improvised moments with these poems and their own musical response. I have more recently been reading excerpts from these poems with Lucian Ban and Mat Maneri, with Mat Maneri's Ash Quartet, and with Marco Cappelli's Italian Surf Academy.

***Ennio Morricone is Dissolving*** is a suite of poems, which began as individual, related poems with composer Ennio Morrione as a subject. Unbeknownst to me when I first started writing these poems, Marco Cappelli had been working with Italian Surf Academy on a number of Morricone's pieces. Cappelli and I first collaborated on these Ennio Morricone poems as a duet and have since performed them many times with Italian Surf Academy, in various cities, in Manhattan and Brooklyn, and in the studio for an album we recorded on 45th Parallel Records in early 2024.

In 2023, Mat Maneri recorded the second record in a series (*Dust … Ash … Mist*) with his quartet (himself on viola, Lucian Ban on piano, John Hébert on bass, and Randy Peterson on drums). Maneri asked me to write the liner notes for *Ash*. After many attempts to write, in prose, about the record, I wrote and gave him my poetry reactions to the work, which Maneri decided were the "liner notes" he wanted. We have since gone on to perform these poems (with the touring quartet – Brandon Lopez replacing Hébert on bass and in trio form with Maneri and Ban) with numbers from the album and from *Dust* in concerts in New York, Pittsburgh, Brooklyn, New Orleans, and elsewhere.

***It's not the olympics*** premiered in collaboration at Barbès in Brooklyn, August 2024 with Marc Ribot on electric guitar, Marco Cappelli on acoustic guitar, and JT Lewis on drums, as an excerpt with Rezo Kiknadze and translator Manana Matiashvili, in Tbilisi, Georgia.

## about the author

**Denver Butson** frequently works with improvisational and chamber jazz musicians and has performed, toured, and recorded this work in various configurations with Mat Maneri, Marco Cappelli, Lucian Ban, Italian Surf Academy, JT Lewis, and Marc Ribot. Butson has exhibited his own visual work and his dialogues/collaborations with visual artists, including Maria Mercedes Martinez/Saha, Karen Revis, Cedric N. Chatterley, and others. Praised by such notable writers as Edmund White, Jim Harrison, Billy Collins, Zoë Ryder White, Tomaž Šalamun, Agha Shahid Ali, Ilya Kaminsky, and W. S. Merwin, Butson has published several books of poetry, some in collaboration with visual artists. His latest book, *The Scarecrow Alibis*, won The Vern Rutsala Poetry Prize and was published by Cloudbank Books in 2022. In 2020 he won the William Matthews Poetry Prize (*Asheville Poetry Review*), judged by Ilya Kaminksky. His work has been featured on National Public Radio and in the Library of Congress's Poetry 180 program (curated by then US Poet Laureate Billy Collins). Butson's poems, writes National Book Award Winner Colum McCann, "knock our comfortable balance all to hell, and then they help stitch our imaginations back together again." He lives with his wife and daughter in Brooklyn, New York.

THE BODILY PRESS
bodilypress.bandcamp.com